LIVE KNOWING LIFE

BOOKS BY MARTIN JANELLO

LIVE KNOWING LIFE
ISBN 978-0-9910649-6-0 (Paperback)
ISBN 978-0-9983020-2-7 (Kindle)

LOVE KNOWING LOVE
ISBN 978-0-9910649-7-7 (Paperback)
ISBN 978-0-9983020-3-4 (Kindle)

PINE KNOWING PAIN
ISBN 978-0-9910649-5-3 (Paperback)
ISBN 978-0-9983020-6-5 (Kindle)

SHINE KNOWING SHAME
ISBN 978-0-9983020-4-1 (Paperback)
ISBN 978-0-9983020-7-2 (Kindle)

CLIMB KNOWING AIM
ISBN 978-0-9983020-5-8 (Paperback)
ISBN 978-0-9983020-8-9 (Kindle)

KNOWING WON'T LET DARKNESS REIGN
ISBN 978-0-9983020-1-0 (Paperback)
ISBN 978-0-9983020-9-6 (Kindle)

PHILOSOPHY OF HAPPINESS
ISBN 978-0-9910649-0-8 (Hardcover)
ISBN 978-0-9910649-8-4 (Paperback, Pt. 1)
ISBN 978-0-9910649-9-1 (Paperback, Pt. 2)
ISBN 978-0-9910649-1-5 (PDF E-book)
ISBN 978-0-9910649-2-2 (Kindle)
ISBN 978-0-9910649-3-9 (EPUB)

PHILOSOPHIC REFLECTIONS
ISBN 978-0-9910649-4-6 (PDF E-book)

LIVE KNOWING LIFE

PHILOSOPHICAL QUOTES & POEMS

MARTIN JANELLO

Copyright © 2015 by Martin Janello
All rights reserved

No part of this book may be reproduced or transmitted,
in any form or by any means, electronic,
mechanical, or otherwise,
without prior written permission from its copyright owner

Cover, book design, and artwork by Martin Janello

Published by Palioxis Publishing

Palioxis, Palioxis Publishing,
and the Palioxis Publishing colophon
are trademarks owned by Martin Janello

Publisher website:
www.palioxis.com

Book website:
www.philosophyofhappiness.com

ISBN 978-0-9910649-6-0

First Edition

CONTENTS

I. PHILOSOPHY — 1

II. HAPPINESS AND PAIN — 15

III. HUMAN AND NATURE — 41

IV. TRUTH AND DECEPTION — 73

V. GOOD AND EVIL — 109

VI. WANDERING MIND — 127

VII. KNOWLEDGE — 143

VIII. PRINCIPLES — 157

IX. LIFE AND DEATH — 185

X. FREEDOM — 201

This book is dedicated

to

those who are

contemplating the world

and their place in it

I.
PHILOSOPHY

I. PHILOSOPHY

Our insides and surroundings provoke unconsidered behavior. Philosophy can educate us to not be a slave to impulses.

Instant requirements for philosophy by humanity are due to the survival and loss of instincts, the rise of technology, and increases in number.

The most widely relevant inquiries of philosophy are about purpose for individuals, societies, and humanity and adjustments toward purpose.

An important question we must ask and answer in philosophy is what we fear and hope to find in its pursuit. Motivations can influence outcome.

Unpracticed philosophy is worthless. To improve, we must assess insights and their applications in an entirety, mend incongruities, and fill gaps.

The purpose of communicating philosophy is to create commonality in views so commonality in conduct or at least tolerance can result.

I. PHILOSOPHY

Humanity may only pay attention to philosophy after transcending its struggle to survive and make a living. However, that may be too late.

The civilization of a society can be measured by how much philosophers are integrated and by how much they are questioned.

Philosophy is a rickety construct that only still stands because it has not been used much and work on it has become so slight and lightweight.

You know a society is troubled when "philosophy" is appropriated by sport coaching, product marketing, and religion, or to describe an attitude.

It is predictable yet shameful how famous, wealthy, or other people in power are deemed by themselves and others philosophical authorities.

Blaming philosophy for not being consumed is like blaming food for not being eaten. But maybe people do not have a taste for what they need.

I. PHILOSOPHY

Philosophers' inability, lack of care, or avoidance to be lucid has burdened generations of disciples laboring to sort out their failures.

Studying philosophy is taking ghost trains through the justifications of psyches that successfully impressed others with their assumptions.

The greatest problem in academic philosophy is that poorly defined special terms and languages scuttle efforts to expose or promote truth.

Philosophy gave birth to science in its search for knowledge. Upon the splitting of specialty sciences, its remaining field has been underlying science as well as the comprehension and arrangement of human existence.

Born to a world of superstitions and restricted freedom of expression, philosophy addressing human existence often compromised its self-declared mandate of pursuing knowledge. Yet even as these confines subsided, it has largely restricted itself to its historical administration and to sophistries without import.

I. PHILOSOPHY

Current academic philosophy is failing humanity by smugly ruminating its historical incidents without resolving to advance.

regurgitating and comparing irrelevant philosophies
tenured charades of education

Thinking philosophy started with writing is an insult to the intelligence of our forbears and ignores the scourge of sophistry that vocal expression can avoid and reveal.

Denying help to the needy adds to their suffering. Does this make institutionalized philosophy responsible, or has it nothing to give?

What is the required or resulting mindset of teaching philosophy with the prospect that nothing much will come of it but its own tradition?

Many philosophy scholars are not philosophers, but merely trying to comprehend and explain what philosophers have conceived.

I. PHILOSOPHY

Researchers and teachers of extant philosophy are as much philosophers as historians are explorers, although one does not exclude the other.

Teaching other people's philosophies makes you as much a philosopher as preaching makes you a god.

Institutional philosophy is rationally disguised religion complete with gods, priests, dogmas, seminaries, confirmations, ordinations, contests and arrangements by denominations.

philosophy professors
reviewers of writings
and reviews of writings
reviewed
by other reviewers

The philosophical gravy train
populated by mutually congratulating
conductors will stop running when
those enabling it ask for results.

If knowledge induces humbleness
about how much remains unknown,
academic arrogance is self-revealing.

I. PHILOSOPHY

those who think
they should teach
rather than learn
have reached their limit

By evading its obligations in human discourse, philosophy concedes its stage to charlatans, self-important incompetents, and demagogues.

At best, haphazard, topical fixes have spanned the voids left by philosophy's delinquencies in developing workable concepts for human existence.

The blind state of humans exhibits itself by their dismissing the necessity or even utility of guiding philosophy.

People reject distant or erroneous philosophies and in disgust do not follow any. Developing their own philosophy could fill this opening.

The pervasive neglect by professional philosophy to assist in understanding and organizing human existence, but also the demands of those tasks, call for profound individual engagement.

II.
HAPPINESS
AND
PAIN

II. HAPPINESS AND PAIN

Happiness arises from overcoming unhappy feelings or circumstances, not from ignoring them.

One of the greatest hindrances in achieving happiness is carrying false imaginations of its conditions.

Human happiness is in flow because it builds and disintegrates in function of external and internal conditions reflecting on the fulfillment of needs. It also requires flow by its even more inhibitory inherently fleeting nature.

We cannot be truly happy without all we naturally care for being happy. To secure happiness short of this scope, we craft emotional causes not to care.

Every renouncement of our need for the happiness of our world punishes us with additional unhappiness.

we wish for happiness
like we dream of heaven
deeming it to be understood
without ascertaining
its principles or ideals

II. HAPPINESS AND PAIN

Grasping happiness transcends improving how we feel. It is an essential condition for individual and collective survival and thriving.

Anybody claiming a simple recipe for reaching and maintaining happiness is wrong. Happiness pertains to and encompasses all our wants and needs.

All our behavior beyond reflexes is motivated by a desire to enhance or maintain happiness. This makes it our most important subject.

Conducting ourselves as if happiness were not the most important good shows how little we comprehend its guiding and regulating functions.

Happiness requires effort. It results from a balance of needs and their pursuits that must be attained and maintained every day.

It is important for us and humanity to take happiness more seriously than following trivial, sporadic, or possibly misleading handling that abounds.

II. HAPPINESS AND PAIN

To be happy, we need more than dribbles of truisms, cute imagery, or hacks. We must look beyond easy fixes and bring our life in order.

Happiness involves more than some steps, mottos, niceties, exhortations, or anecdotes. It calls for all-inclusive consideration, preferably by us.

I have high hopes for virtual organic farming because so much being said, written, or thought about happiness can cover its natural fertilizer needs.

happiness
key of life
trivialized
by money power self-promotion
or naive whistling in the dark

Many sellers of happiness advice tell
people what they want to hear,
thereby deepening their failure to
face reality and resulting problems.

to be happy
we must know
its contrast

II. HAPPINESS AND PAIN

We require distress to understand and act upon what is important. Hence, those trying to keep us calm may not have our interests in mind.

Only after we leave childish beliefs, superstitions, and fairy tales behind can we competently understand, devise, and address our happiness.

Humans will continue in a sorry state until they realize that the happiness of their surroundings is essential for their happiness and act accordingly.

Humanity and humans can only achieve optimal happiness when they leave nobody and nothing behind.

The most pernicious human idea is that happiness can be obtained from the abuse or exclusion of our human or more extended environment.

The decrease of community building and reinforcing tasks in human development impedes happiness. Retaining and advancing positive tribal mechanisms is essential.

II. HAPPINESS AND PAIN

Our quest for happiness has a dark, destructive side that emerges from frustration when we cannot achieve satisfaction but also after we reach it.

Lifestyle and attitude changes may not have us deal with the fundamental precepts of happiness. They can resemble reseeding a toxic waste site with wildflowers.

Many resist questioning their ways or having them questioned, even if they are unhappy, for fear of ensuing pain.

Happiness derives from harmonizing internal and external conditions. Yet we only possess limited powers, and much remains beyond our control.

We can overcome our consideration and dedication deficits and improve happiness by becoming aware of ourselves and our surroundings.

Happiness quotes exemplify that sounding clever or comforting does not make us right and that being right may not make a difference.

II. HAPPINESS AND PAIN

Emanating from fulfillment events of
our needs and their approximations,
happiness must be continually
earned, permitting only brief reposes.

Every worthwhile achievement forms
a means in the pursuit of another.

she's like a house
built to be filled
with happy life
yet she is mostly reserved
for occasions not realized
and people never present

happiness lies in little things
but also in greater circumstances
it can be found and lost in everything
because everything is connected to us

Happiness arises in moments of
ultimate achievement, but also in its
anticipation during advancement,
each step being its own achievement.

unspeakable sadness befalls me
learning what humans have done
to one another and their settings
in the name of happiness

II. HAPPINESS AND PAIN

The principle of happiness unfolds in harmonic development of and among personal existence, humanity, and the more extended environment. It is the organizing principle of nature.

We may shut others out of our considerations of happiness if we take advantage of them or fear compassion would infect us with their pain. In either event, we ask our mind to fabricate justifications we can apply as veneers to our conscience. Still, underneath we conceive our harm to the potential of self-reflective and mutually supportive happiness.

We often choose erroneous objectives or manners of pursuit because we are told by unenlightened minds that these constitute aspects of happiness.

If currently practiced doctrines of happiness are truthful, why are so many of their practitioners and subjects of their practices desolate?

Human unhappiness is self-inflicted by ignorance and error. Its remedy is the development and implementation of confirmed principles of happiness.

II. HAPPINESS AND PAIN

Because life is difficult, peddlers of simple, ultimately faulty solutions find plenty of takers.

In personal development, we can tweak the status quo, or we can examine and optimize our life.

incessantly startled
no way out to see
only his nightmares
made him feel heartened
that in his sleep
he could fight or flee

Pursuing superficial and unsystematic
fixes to happiness and giving in to
their marketing tragically keep us
from advancing and may set us back.

reality right before our eyes
yet we're set refusing to see
we could make the world paradise
instead of blind hell's fantasy

we try to drown out
the undertone pain
of living in doubt
and loving in vain

II. HAPPINESS AND PAIN

a look

like a

lightening

of the soul

Maybe the world is in such a decrepit state because our thresholds for pain are too high or we do not address its causes despite substantial motivation.

Some create trouble, even if they can expect it to cause them pain, to obscure other pain they cannot or do not wish to address.

be aware be there

explore create share

pain follows disconnection

the asphalt still shows

a gaping gash

where she was taken

in a crash

some wounds never heal

much pain arises from

missing belief in humanity

and its justification in fact

can we become better by resolve

II. HAPPINESS AND PAIN

Many deserve their misery because they are unwilling to change themselves or their circumstances.

Happiness remains hampered while we willingly suffer abuse to fuel imaginary or temporary escapes.

We settle into painful settings.

Take comfort knowing that straight lines can be uninteresting.

some happiness is

less in arrival

but travel

less in order

than unravel

Some happiness derives from partial aspects, but greater happiness flows from a comprehensive approach.

Distinguishing the grief we suffer due to our disposition and behavior from externally incurred pain is important to improve our situation.

II. HAPPINESS AND PAIN

normal persons are

well adjusted to the world

but what if their world is crazy

nightmares suppressed

keep edging up

searching for weakness to break

tender membrane

of daytime rest

proving our consciousness fake

sadness and anger

are reactions to pain

its causes are the problems

When I was young, I could not stand sensations moving me beyond my control. Grownups build tolerances. There are good and bad sides to this.

Are painful circumstances improving, or are we ignoring them better?

much human suffering
comes from facts
but vastly more from
lacking information
refusal to acknowledge
and misrepresentation

II. HAPPINESS AND PAIN

every tear is a tear
in the fabric of our soul
we must try to heal

old man jack
never greeted back
his problem jerk
but then i thought again
imagined his pain
more than my hurt

surrounded by cruelty
we are afraid to find out
for fear of not being able to forget

Happiness comes from constructive movement and harmony. Music gives us impressions of this.

when shock reigns
fire and ice clash
in our veins
debilitating rush

Happiness is impossible without awareness of pain as a defining contrast. Resolving the contradiction of pain as foe and constructive requirement is our challenge.

III. HUMAN AND NATURE

III. HUMAN AND NATURE

an endless seashore
our footsteps erased
by ebb and flow in time
can we escape

cradled by a meadow
giggles
infinity
framed by grasses and flowers

If other living entities could talk,
their designation for the worst
behavior and their worst swear word
for one another would be "human."

Raping our mother, nature, destroys not only our sourcing. It also makes us loathe ourselves and one another and crave and pursue punishment.

Humanity acts as a disease on the world ecosystem. Impenitently high opinions of ourselves worsen our virulence and quicken its and our fall.

the flower
in the concrete desert
gives me hope
and hopelessness

III. HUMAN AND NATURE

claiming to be spirits
we renounce nature
as our mother
and kill her children

imagine humans
as growing conducts
representing life
what they can effect
and what can happen to them

we spend ourselves one another
and our nonhuman environment
for attainments we don't need

rose-clouded dawn
pelican flaps its wings
in oil slick one last time

Rights are defined by a harmony of needs. Accordingly, humans have rights, but so do most other living organisms. The supremely defining force is the logic of advancing nature.

Soon we will have to decide whether to limit technological progress or to merge with it. Its many irresistible incremental benefits favor the latter.

III. HUMAN AND NATURE

Technology is enabling us to learn, connect, and advance in many ways. It also threatens to insulate, distract, misinform, and violate us. Judicious use of it is therefore imperative.

Replacing human with machine interactions may appear to relieve us from ethics toward machines and in machine applications. Temptations for inhumane regression abound.

Humanity is childishly trying to find independence from its parent.

Failure to understand humanity's path according to its genesis and setting in nature causes disharmony and threatens its chances of success.

Being a self-conscious cusp of nature, our responsibilities for it are extreme.

Treating nature and its constituents as living entities seems to be a helpful mental construct in humanity's self-interest for managing harmonious interaction. This may also correspond to present or future factualities.

III. HUMAN AND NATURE

Albeit reluctantly, we are more likely
to recognize extraordinary qualities
deemed typical to humans in animals
than to admit animal traits in us.

you have not lived
until you have walked a forest
in a summer rain

he said he liked it
in the wilderness
escaping human judgment
even his own
to be measured by nature

nature addresses

unredressed offenses

hope after all

though maybe not for us

moon sun stars

views of earthly nature

help us forget our human mess

nature is coming alive

passing its achievements

to new generations

that advance its mission

of transforming itself

III. HUMAN AND NATURE

humans
turning earth
into dirt

our highest ideal
is to be
pursuant to our nature
in nature
yet we struggle
understanding either
and reconciling them

the microbes used the microscope
to look humans deep in the eyes

walls floors ceilings
fences closing in
we are made to
embrace nature
and be held in her embrace

we all are flowers
from the same earth
and so easily affected

Originating from, living on, and
returning to nature annoys our fragile
ego. Malcontent and arrogant, we
deny communion and seek distance.

III. HUMAN AND NATURE

We debase nature by claiming against
overwhelming evidence she could not
have created us, at least not entirely,
because we believe we are too special.

Rejecting obvious natural progression
from humble beginnings, we invent
to have been created by supernatural
beings conceitedly deemed akin to us.

a machine pulling trees
like carrots
environmentally friendly
since there is no waste

in humanity
nature has an opportunity
to become constructively conscious
or to go insane
which way it will go seems uncertain

Most humans appear to be sedated or distracted by themselves or by others to not address reality.

If we do not understand and face reality, how can we successfully mend deficiencies, preserve the worthwhile, and effectively or efficiently advance?

III. HUMAN AND NATURE

We all carry a dangerous hierarchic remnant of evolution, which makes us assume that prevailing individuals or groups are right and defer to them.

Humanity can transform itself and nature into higher forms of existence. Yet proper vision and execution are vital to avoid dangerous pitfalls.

imagine a time when humans roamed
simpler closer to who we are
artifice made us a threat to our own
without changing we will not get far

Many sports are ritualized, disguised war, rousing the lowest instincts into shamefully hostile displays. Witness the wording, emotions, and conduct.

Regardless of whether our universe expands and contracts or eventually dissipates, human existence is ultimately pointless unless we change or transcend either limitation.

animals and plants
can give us many lessons
about the joy of life

III. HUMAN AND NATURE

Human rights are founded on mutual recognition of human needs. The only question left is whether they include assistance to those in need.

Humanity continues to be steeped in its primitive beginnings and their crazed distortions. Realizing this is the sole path to betterment and perhaps the key to its survival.

humanity
floating in space
without much of a concept

Asking whether humanity is getting dumber or just applying itself less may be pointless because applying ourselves less may make us dumber.

Status: We struggle progressing to a level where humanity proves itself worth saving and promoting, even in its own assessment.

Our primitive adherences to exclusive tribality and to hierarchy are major obstacles to peace and justice and account for most of human misery.

III. HUMAN AND NATURE

watchers shake heads
and settle their bets
humanity is gone

Now more than ever our social position is defined by who will or won't communicate with us. This reinforces hierarchies and exclusive tribalities on a pervasive scale.

Human circumstances are slow to change because most of us want to be confirmed, not challenged in our ways or are uncertain of alternatives.

I see many tales of injustice, but a lot less realization of why circumstances are unjust, the causes of injustice, and how they can be counteracted.

If we were smart enough, we would be humble enough about our lack of wisdom, skill, and fortitude to tread lightly and keep alternatives open.

Think what humanity could achieve with the energies wasted by personal confusion, social injustice, violence, and misdirected pain management.

III. HUMAN AND NATURE

Reducing our sensory receptions, considerations, and discussions to bits renders us unsteady and pliable. Is this not increasingly our reality?

If we want to progress, we must overcome our technologically induced attention deficit. Will our faculties catch up with the potentials and developments of information?

information society
mining selling and control
great ideas drowning in idle chatter

Do you think conceiving and formulating great ideas is hard? Try getting people to pay attention to them. We live in an attention deficit world in which the flashiest win.

The internet calls on us to evolve to be more aware, thoughtful, and caring. This may result in a sensory, cognitive, and emotional network.

clay tablets to electrons
human memorialization
becomes a fruit fly

III. HUMAN AND NATURE

Social media are upgrades to communicating through Morse code. Eventually, we must emerge from isolation and act to effect change.

We should fear aware machines not only because they may lack human emotions but also because they may notice our reckless practice thereof.

living naturally
secret wish while mired
in bounds deformities and crutches
we can only go forward

Speed-reading, memory, and other brain improvements are essential for humans to remain in charge of aptly applying expanding areas of required and other beneficial information.

body language
lost signals
in the age of word messaging

In spite of our development, we are primates, and the most emotionally effective form of communication remains touch or its absence.

III. HUMAN AND NATURE

we follow one another
to the same destination
why not during our existence
for us and humanity
common legacy
of a live window traveling
through time and space

words branding our souls
we are set to become
what parents said we are

hope for survival
despite our stupidity

if there were love

who could stand it

if there were truth

who would want it

if there were hope

who would seek it

not made for zen

we think feel want

more than we have

humans wreck perfection

because it leaves them

without pursuit

III. HUMAN AND NATURE

the world is like a theater
most watch some build the set
some play and few direct

raised to function
channel feelings
into accepted aggression
and silent suffering
sacrificing
warrior or
worker ant

humans create conditions
they then want to forget

many rest and abuse

upon reaching higher levels

instead of serving

crimes of prior generations

are decomposing many lands

their profit should give us

trepidations

there will be no justice

without amends

Despite reflective capacities, most humans give in to be governed by the whims of primitive instincts.

III. HUMAN AND NATURE

progressing numbers
of days lived
we become jaded
in expectations
what can happen

the world we get
when we let
overinflated egos
one-track minds
psychopaths
profiteers
tricksters
and charlatans
run its affairs
is this

The ignorant, feeble of mind, fearful,
speculating, delusional, hallucinating,
unbalanced, avaricious, and cynical
keep determining humanity's course.

are there enough
to understand to feel
that we are one
i often fear
words and deeds will fade
and nothing will be won

Ignorance and arrogance lead us to
deny human nature is part of nature.

III. HUMAN AND NATURE

much going wrong
we could make it right
if we would just stop
our flight or fight

a time when loyalty
was reserved to brands
and corporate machines
were ruled to be people

we may be able to
love think do enough
to eliminate conflict
but how can we get there

guiltily quiet we become naming
negative aspects of human nature

Does humanity have enough interest
to find a path to a better world, and
does it have sufficient motivation and
discipline to walk it?

we rise without waking
expand without growing
spend without earning
judge without knowing
commit without loving
and die without living

IV.
TRUTH
AND
DECEPTION

IV. TRUTH AND DECEPTION

one can tell a lot from hands

how they look

how they move

how they touch

all we can do

is share our truth

and hope it resonates

trust in human communion

People and peoples who mythologize their history, present, or future are attempting to compensate for their problems recognizing the truth.

Reality contradicts claims that we are
perfect as we are - but it also contains
encouraging indications of our
potential to become much better.

the world might take
a quantum leap
if people heeded their advice

affirmations
we are good enough as we are
lies keeping us
from mending and advancing beyond
but we like absolution

IV. TRUTH AND DECEPTION

not all we are is perfect
not all criticism wrong
build strength to consider this

How can we be happy if we cling to
fake excuses why we should ignore
the plight of fellow humans? We
cannot wash off the smell of our lies.

Our problem is timidity and
disingenuity. To cloak our fear and
guard superficial benefits, we pretend
waiting for inspiration to do what we
already know to be right.

How much time and energy do we spend hiding, suppressing, or diverting our wishes compared to making them come true?

The use of mood altering drugs in a society is proportional to how unbearable it is for members to live in it without suspension of reality.

People will suspend their critical judgment and invest themselves in nonsense if it helps them contain concerns or address other ambitions.

IV. TRUTH AND DECEPTION

We say something rings true if it resonates with our inclinations or tenets. But how did these receive their tuning?

Have you noticed how often matters, when closely examined, are not only different from but the opposite of what powerful interests claim?

Opening individuals to themselves can be more difficult than having them follow someone else. We like being collected in our shells.

I have (not) become, I am (not), I may (not) become, I will (not) have been . . . . Write and finish these sentences. This is you - or is it?

Forgetting and falsifying history are the only ways humanity can live with itself short of changing. Victors prolong their avoidance of truth.

Einstein's pithy criticisms of human nature seem ironic considering he kept urging nuclear weapons research that enabled Hiroshima/Nagasaki.

IV. TRUTH AND DECEPTION

Some people insist the world is black
and white while they can see color
and there is firm evidence for
frequencies beyond their perception.

calm assurances
all would be fine
even if nothing was
insight beyond
or asinine lies

there are more important things
than finding harmony
our demons whisper

with each changing season

they childishly trusted

war would be vanquished

by rhythms of life

the news

part of an effort

to make us sad

to make us feel

the world is bad

a noose

to choke us

so we agree

to give up

and bow

to authority

IV. TRUTH AND DECEPTION

lies by omission
and characterization
while making us think
we are well informed

sleeplessness is not wakefulness
some pursue it to feel
the numbing pall of drowsiness

much of our life
we waste hanging in
hoping for things to get better
stalling afraid of change setting in
avoiding to be a change setter

come away with me

to be free

in the living room of nature

caves were merely meant

for protection

people and societies

are usually the opposite

of what they brag to be

Ideologies lay their insecurities bare

by preventing their subjects from

questioning doctrines and by taking

offense in questioning from others.

IV. TRUTH AND DECEPTION

truths we gladly reveal
some we'd like to
perceive think or feel
but then there's what we dare not tell
for shame or scorn or fear of hell

humanity has squandered
most of its efforts and dignity
on wild speculations and delusions

Fairy tales grownups believe are as absurd as those they tell children. But they are better shaping circumstances according to their pretenses.

truth

can bear

doubt

Personal development evangelists
claiming unseen that you are great
when you know you are not. How
long can the diversion last?

i will never get used to
how set people are in their ways
how they shirk
exploring answers to questions
that torture them all their life

IV. TRUTH AND DECEPTION

people demonstrating
how powerful they are
trying to get past
how small they feel

compensating weakness
snake pit of betrayal and posturing
conceding truth brings betterment

We must carefully consider whether to emphasize the positive over the negative. It may distract and dissuade us from grasping negative conditions and from properly addressing them.

pieces of advice
people give others
may have fallen off
rotting carcasses
spun by
the careening carousel
of their ego

self-importance
opposite of intelligence
mistaken for it by fools

No other frailty has damaged
humankind more than gullibility.

IV. TRUTH AND DECEPTION

kicking bitter truths
and embracing sweet lies
will leave us askew

Pretension causes tension.

idiocies believed by many
become conventional wisdom

shouting danger
on a raft heading for a fall
invites ire from the oblivious

A problematic quality of many statements is that their truth depends on the circumstances.

Our childhood ends when we find out about the past and present failings of grownups. Thus, every generation must deal with disappointment.

numbing or denying realities
we cannot bear
prevents human development
we must stare grief in the eyes
until it flinches

IV. TRUTH AND DECEPTION

buying illusions of happiness
we know
they are fake
but close our mind
scared to awake

giving ourselves
too much credit
makes us live in debt
and anticipation of collection

False education is more dangerous
than mere ignorance because it is
defended by pride.

deceptions may convince others
but we always know
we're just playing a show

claiming the opposite
of what we perceive think or feel
indicates desire for distance
devil's advocate
trying to believe
nothing is wrong

empty words
give us some time
to call them aspirations

IV. TRUTH AND DECEPTION

Many spend their life trying to prove the same assertions over and over, often without an end. Even if they should convince others, they may not succeed believing themselves.

see all these people
running and clawing
to get distance from themselves
while claiming to seek who they are

being true to yourself
can be painful
for exterior and interior reasons

Accounts driven by agendas may miss shades. But fabrications, omissions, and mischaracterizations by guiding authorities should be unforgivable.

We are conditioned to a state in which very little that should outrage us can break our apathy. Even this fact does not appear to bother us.

We live in a mendacious world where assuming the opposite of what institutions and persons would like us to believe is a necessary safeguard.

IV. TRUTH AND DECEPTION

life becomes genuine
after dropping our
coveralls of pretenses
though we may
struggle in settings
resenting naked truth

allowing events
to knock us senseless
calling results zen

masks we wear
while we look in the mirror
simmering under facades

pretending things are fine

when they are not

protective cowardice

fueled by fears of

disconnection exclusion

and falling prey

many people ask for truth

but after a peek at it

prefer the cover of shams

we may be denying

our ice floe is melting

for fear of losing our ground

IV. TRUTH AND DECEPTION

we are all
just old children
acting like grownups

manipulations
and bets
instead of substance
nonproductive participants
must be paid

advertising
politics
and religion
prove gullibility

only her front
would be good enough
in trying to shape her future
sacrifice truth for living a dream

some people disown
whom they left behind
as witnesses of who they were

she assembled her persona
so they would
neither see through her
nor see her
leaving her a respected enigma

IV. TRUTH AND DECEPTION

our views

are not truth

only our opinions of it

quietly suffering

they were told later

they should have spoken up

but one who did

was called troublemaker

and persecuted to shut him up

we like to hide

behind interpretations

till reality punches through

agitation and screams
about unreal importance
tranquilizing distractions
or preparations of sports

telling stories
he set the world free
trustworthiness of apparent lies

Religions were devised to hold
primitives in check and direct them.
They still fall on fertile ground in
those and in people who do not trust
individual or collective discernment.

IV. TRUTH AND DECEPTION

Religions thrive on fear of death and the unknown, and if people are too stupid, impulsive, or careless to devise harmonious, principled lives.

Picture humanity if we based our conduct on findings rather than beliefs and on our determination to use our faculties to their best effect.

Pantheons of heaven, hell, gods, devils, angels, demons and their undertakings are very real. They are externalizations of inner beings.

Many religious individuals and sects judge beliefs of others harshly while hypocritically discounting that they themselves cling to far-out fairy tales.

One of the worst exploitations is taking advantage of the spiritual needs of others. Then again, it is their fault as well for being such fools.

Hell on earth is not surprising if people derive ethics and laws from religions that allow crimes ordered, committed, or forgiven by a god.

IV. TRUTH AND DECEPTION

Beware of "spiritual" nonsense posing as philosophy. Philosophy is fearless desire for knowledge wherever it may lead, not a flight into make-believe.

They say human search for love is due to an addiction to chemically induced highs our body produces in reaction to certain stimulants. Should we favor sobriety or manage our addiction?

what people want to hear
is obscenely more popular
than what they need to hear

Reality is there to be evidenced if we dare to look at it and quit childishly believing stories that distract from it. Partial reality does not redeem them.

If humans would stop making life hell for themselves and one another, they could die in peace and would not have to hope for a better afterlife.

Why do we believe in nonsense? The potential for happiness in reality is awesome enough. If we would only respect, explore, and actualize it.

IV. TRUTH AND DECEPTION

The Dark Ages have not yet ended. The world is still suffocating in the strangleholds of superstition, lack of enlightenment, and resulting malice.

We can only come into our own by recognizing no god is interceding and all we have is one another, the rest of nature, and the future.

The problem with successful ruthless or lucky people is often their conviction that their positive attributes brought them this far.

Too many people could not care less about us unless we matter in their nearsighted plans. This may make them swindlers in social displays.

Humans create unnecessarily harsh conditions. To address them, we must comprehend them, question asserted causes, and imagine alternatives.

afraid of the facts about cats and mice
and what these might entail
they decided to live entrapped in lies
assisting the scheme not to fail

IV. TRUTH AND DECEPTION

Truth is never ugly even if it conveys circumstances we'd rather not have occur. It innocently and loyally points to causes for offenses that we must understand if we are to resolve them.

looking for reasons
after we act
proves us blind
and prejudiced

truths are simple
we complicate
to excuse not heeding them

unable to find ourselves
we may take on shapes
disguising we don't know who we are

i live in the mirror
beyond the pane
where semblances dare not go
out here i am superficial and vain
hoping my faults will not show

masked by compassion righteousness
or mere informational concerns
many seek solace
in hardships of others

V. GOOD AND EVIL

V. GOOD AND EVIL

knowing us
caring like no other
offering guidance and support
judging and punishing us
for ignoring its commands
conscience is our natural god

Taking advantage of a forgiving
attitude is difficult to forgive because
its cynicism causes great struggle in
victims to preserve purity.

in dysfunctional settings
the dysfunctional succeed

if we all take

whatever we can

nothing will be left

of us

arrogant fools

self-enforcing agents

of karma

virtue requires

close attention

to its effects

unreconciled principles

may yield evil

V. GOOD AND EVIL

Stripping history of exclusive tribal
and of hierarchic justifications reveals
human cruelty crushing life and love.

many years later
not hot anymore
she still thinks
she can judge me
and make me feel bad

be positive docile
trust all will be well
give evil a license
to take you to hell

Engaging in unilateral, but rejection of bilateral, communications by persons who are deemed important by themselves or by others is ignorant, arrogant, and uncaring.

All too often the problem is not that individuals lack a sense of right, but that they decide to ignore it. They fulfill the definition of evil.

Those identifying themselves with the loftiest characteristics frequently possess the lowest.

V. GOOD AND EVIL

Definitions of positive and negative may omit essential evaluations in the context of our entirety. A lack of sensory, intellectual, or emotional awareness may lead us astray.

Criminals winning a war by misdeeds are rewarded by their tribes with monuments and citations for heroic virtues and wisdom. Their wrongs are denied, justified, or downplayed.

Evil eagerly camouflages itself with the mantle of legitimacy.

There is a promoted assumption that victorious forces in history are good when they may only be favored by luck, extraneous circumstances, or a more calculating focus on power.

Institutions and officials responsible for the murder, torture, and misery of countless humans keep evading justice and continue to be indulged.

Shocking how evil committed in the name of gods or their followers gains acceptability and even admiration.

V. GOOD AND EVIL

When we injure humans or allow them to be injured, our conscience rebels and exhorts us. This is part of a general reactive mechanism. If our conscience does not limit or correct the devastation we commit or permit, the consequences eventually will.

Not putting anybody down
elevates us.

self-involved humans
ignoring or harming others
a sliding scale of evil

People resent reporting one's own good deeds. Yet this together with tracking one another's good deeds may significantly improve conditions.

don't talk to me
about peace you found
until all injustice is mended

As long as nations get away with crimes that, if committed by other groups or individuals, would warrant punishment, international law remains a farce played by the strong.

V. GOOD AND EVIL

Cultures that discourage deep consideration are sinister, foolish, or both. We give up if we count on benefiting from ignorant alignment.

deprived mantra
never give up
privileged mantra
never give down
unless you must

everything good
whispers opposite potential
we can never be at peace

i'd rather be wrong

than righteous

arrogance of perfection

beware of those who champion

acceptance over truth

don't let them inherit the earth

On the wicked words are wasted.

Not identifying or acting against

injustice makes us guilty of it.

V. GOOD AND EVIL

justice for banksters

share the loot

and go on to scheme another day

easing children

into grownup schemes

controlling their revulsion

happy

some want the world to be happy

sad

some want the world to be sad

dying

some want the world to end

Discrimination stems from fear for position. It stops when it provokes sufficient threat to position.

In their quest for distinction few can resist diminishing others.

bullying and conformism
underhanded compliments by evil
on independence and authenticity

Humans horrify the world.

V. GOOD AND EVIL

the prudent and decent

yielding

to be trumped

by the brazen and insane

what more will they take

already took most

conceding the rest

to go on taking

all bells rung

tearless anguish

pittance thrown

past hardly opened doors

no mercy for the dirty

cast down the

sewage system of affluence

we are imperfections

and compromises

dreaming of purity

Evil arises from a misalignment
among human needs.

Evil banks on us looking away.

V. GOOD AND EVIL

feeling better
when others feel worse
is an expression of evil

hearts are impure
when they ignore or rejoice in
the suffering of others

The source of social evil is
competition, its antidote cooperation.

Evil is contagious, but so is good.

Evil threatens to pull us into its dominion. Fighting it by matching or exceeding evil methods and lying to distinguish our actions hand evil a victory over the good in us.

As much as we may deny it, we are culpable for ills we do not explore and counteract within our abilities.

The unresponsiveness of individuals and groups unless they have an expectation of direct profit is shamefully cruel and shortsighted.

VI.
WANDERING MIND

VI. WANDERING MIND

memories of being
but what proves
that i or anything was
except what is now
history by deduction

the streams of life
grind us like pebbles
but we are life
able to grow anew

we can start again
if we wish to forgo
resignation's comfort

this was the day

she swore a new start

severed each tendon

anchoring her

even as it meant leaving

parts of her self behind

lost

swirling down to our center

from which we can burst with energy

end of the rope

motivational signal

for reverse motion

VI. WANDERING MIND

Our reality ails from lack of
imagination what it could be.

sadness eats at us
about the past
for two reasons
the passing of
or lack of experiencing
beauty
this view also infects our outlook
in the fear such losses will continue

all we cannot live anymore
remains in regret or yearning

want to break
those calcified ends
make them open and fluid

Time is in front of us and rushes
through us into nothing. Turning
around is then worse than looking
ahead knowing it will end for us.

exhausted in the morning
you wish to go back
into the night
and before
but all you can do is move on

VI. WANDERING MIND

weekend clips of
treasured pleasure
in the shredder of time

The most unforgivable acts in human
existence are neglect, suppression,
and destruction of positive potential.

you share dreams
of beautiful still lives
and stirring events
in neatly bowed parcels
why don't you open
these gifts for yourself

a balanced purposed life requires

remembrance

presence

and future perspective

i know you are tired

and maybe afraid

but time is forever

so nothing's too late

the moon is a mirror

reflecting our dreams

in silhouette kisses

by its ghostly beams

VI. WANDERING MIND

i want to live in a world
where babies would smile
if they knew their life ahead

her flaw
the perfection
of not trying

her dreams kept returning
to a different reality
detailed and complete
so familiar yet so strange
she felt guilty missing it
after waking

the future a theater

waiting for us

we would define our roles

in dreams

i captured you in words

then guiltily set you free

no recall of my poem hurts

but morning

brought you back to me

broken dreams

broken promises

now you must hatch

VI. WANDERING MIND

We may wish to forget what our mind
is working on in dreams because we
may fear we could not function if we
realized and acted out the concerns
of our soul in conscious daylight.

Optimistic, we wish to be disabused
of negative and confirmed in positive
notions. Pessimistic, our preferences
are opposite. Both stances cause bias.

how often do we distort reality
by sensing what we want it to be
or exaggerating discrepancy

We may believe we know ourselves. Yet we only register results of sensory events, thoughts, and emotions, not their processes or mechanisms.

Recalling our past accesses a treasure from which we can draw our present and plan our future. The trick is not letting its weight define us.

We have to overcome approaching our life as if we were not in it. Our sensory and cognitive reflections tend to separate us as observers of our self.

VI. WANDERING MIND

that woman

lying with me

in my dream

never seen her before

she was just here

it seemed so real

she woke me up with her snore

if we'd suspend our gravity

we'd have to call it levity

living our dreams to fly

our ambitions will not rest

until we can fly without help

emotional forces
ignored for too long
grind our insides raw

He felt life was a rehearsal interlaced
with studying, waiting, arguing,
rewriting, and being directed, all
readying for a real performance.

shoes bought
in fantasies of wearing
rows waiting for the right occasions
until she breaks their spell
and dances a barefoot farewell

VI. WANDERING MIND

chiffon wrapped dreams
captured in seams
no nerve to lay them open
she stays laced up for life

as people age
they may lose faith
hope strangled mess
they settle for less

dreams of the past
present or future
reminders of our truth
all too soon forgotten

imagine life without
damage and retreat
from ill circumstances

she held on to
her red shiny dream
until all air had escaped

do you remember
when life was adventure
not just a matter of time
expectations wound up
we missed the bus
now saving for future tolls

VII.
KNOWLEDGE

VII. KNOWLEDGE

We have much yet to know and many long ways to go. Existing knowledge ≠ access ≠ acquisition ≠ application ≠ harmonious use of knowledge.

The challenge for humanity's advancement in the current informational whirlwind is separating kernels of substance from chaff.

if all you knew were darkness
you would not miss light
nor would you miss air as an aquatic
just like before you were born

Lacking clarity in the expression of concepts sets forth an overwhelming presumption that clarity was missing in their cognition as well.

stroke of genius
playfully
stumbling across
what was already there

That we keep believing in a better world despite being serially disabused hints at an intrepid inner knowledge we should bring to light.

VII. KNOWLEDGE

The sole reason we acknowledge something as logical is having witnessed or been told that events habitually work in certain fashions.

People who won't investigate are or become simpletons. They depend on information packaged by elites to whom deep knowledge is reserved.

Genius speaks through simplicity, and striking ideas become obvious once conceived. But what does this say about human intelligence?

In settings of boundless information
sharing possibilities we also share an
increasingly essential responsibility to
refrain from information pollution.

many willfully limit their horizon
afraid to venture beyond
and persecute or ridicule
those who do

The most annoying human weakness
is refusal to acknowledge, much less
seek, evidence in contradiction of
established or desired paradigms.

VII. KNOWLEDGE

The bandwidth of human intelligence is narrow enough to be fathomable. It is also erratic. Smarts in some aspects can coexist with foolishness in others.

I cannot decide whether human existence would benefit or suffer if one could tap into other persons' perceptions, thoughts, and feelings.

cold autumn sundays
they told us children to be sad
ask forgiveness remember dead
we wondered what their problem was

If we cannot comprehend or do something, we tend to rely on others who claim competence without demanding adequate advance proof and subsequent accountability.

are we too busy
focusing on what's next
to weigh its importance
based on what was and is

thought once the world
was black and white
until color was invented

VII. KNOWLEDGE

wanting to find out
and wanting to forget
irresolvable contradiction

If we look up-close into a person's eyes, they become one. Yet we know we are not facing a cyclops. A lesson in the importance of perspective.

We are told and tell ourselves to believe because essential premises of human existence cannot be known. Yet sensory, rational, and emotional facilities increasingly prove this false.

Asking about the beginning of everything creates a paradox since it endlessly begs the question what came before to cause it.

Time is a phenomenon arising from the existence and movement of mass and underlying vibrations. Causation may be limited to these references.

Quantum physics demonstrate that we suffer limits in understanding causation. Breaking these may answer questions about origin and destiny.

VII. KNOWLEDGE

The puzzlingly illogical occurrences of quantum physics teach us that our comprehension of reality's nature is significantly underdeveloped.

As we delve deeper into the nature of nature, our mental grasp weakens together with a dimming of our senses and technological extensions.

Following matter into its details, it dissolves into ever smaller particles and properties. Maybe properties are all there is, and no matter exists.

We know reality mostly on relatively high levels of particle interaction. We claim comprehension because we can name aggregations and observe them following laws, citing mere results.

We do not know the fundamental nature of physical phenomena.

with night flights
past known galaxies
she proved there was no end
just reconnection
we can't understand

VII. KNOWLEDGE

Nonlocal quantum correlations prove time and space are phenomena of the second and third dimensions that reflect an imperfect view of reality.

Our physical and mental captivity in our limited reality does not currently permit us to understand its apparent existence in a setting transcending its basic tenets of time and space.

A deeper, nonlocal and nontemporal nature of the universe has enormous import for our traditional inquiries.

Without separation by distance or time, all exists not at one point and time, but without locality or time. Physical discreteness is an illusion.

Absent physical discreteness does not imply a lack of logic, whose nature is nonlocal and nontemporal. We thus exist in a reality constituted by logic.

We will have to get used to the idea that potential and executed realities are the same without beginning or end. Only our experiences are finite.

VIII.
PRINCIPLES

VIII. PRINCIPLES

Celebrate variety. It would be a poor world if everything and everybody were the same. Differences cause us to learn, even about ourselves.

There is not one person who could not teach us something in some way, if only by negative example. A bonus in our search for cooperation.

It is not difficult to be a good person: Treat others as you would want to be treated in their position and apply your best efforts in helping life.

Coining or acknowledging agreeable sayings is easy. The hard part is placing them into a system of being that makes us want to heed them.

All is flow. Standing still or reversing uses much energy that is neutralized as we are eventually washed along. Steer wisely in the stream.

look at what you lost
learn from it
say goodbye
and move on

VIII. PRINCIPLES

The best advice I ever received was to hold on unless I should let go.

people might not hear you
if you speak
but they certainly won't hear you
if you stay silent
and then the blame is on you

Next time you argue your position, start by exploring and voicing your counterpart's position. The resulting understanding and showing of care assist participants to resolve issues.

individuals helping individuals
individuals helping communities
communities helping individuals
communities helping communities
don't wait for impersonal government

There is no rule without exception,
except that there can be no exception
to this rule if it is to be true.

Conduct must be a cap stone carried
by foundations of sensory, emotional,
and rational considerations of the
past, present, and future.

VIII. PRINCIPLES

When you have more in common with people on social media than acquaintances or friends in your physical life, it is time for change.

believe in yourself
better yet
know yourself

running after people
who do not stop
and turn around
when you call them
is a waste of energy

do not wait do not hate

do not push do not rush

do not grieve do not believe

do not judge do not drudge

do not lie do not stand by

find others

reprogram

the machine

Observe, think, and check your emotions before, while, and after you act. This slows you down but saves enormous time, effort, and pain.

VIII. PRINCIPLES

a drowning man
lessons in swimming
there is a time for everything

Only if we have harmony within us
can harmony with our human and
nonhuman environment develop.

we degrade people from other places
branding them alien or foreign
as if they were not human like us
why don't we call them
visitors or guests
and maybe one day friends

We should be humble. Much is to be
learned or achieved, many limitations
and weaknesses are to be overcome,
and many of our deficits will remain.

do not yield
to interests profiting
from instilling fear

judging people implies
a reasonable requirement
and adequate knowledge
in all other cases
let's give it a rest

VIII. PRINCIPLES

mistaking what we want
for what is
and the reverse
both lead to tragedy

i mourn a culture
when shoes were cared for
to last a lifetime

Frenzying people into believing they can do anything is one of the oldest, most unrealistic, dangerous, and inevitably disheartening forms of manipulation.

living life wisely is not easy

but easier than

bearing it without wisdom

lack of respect

yields resentment

reinforcing ours

and so on

in our still

when we let go

of all trains to hop on

or to watch passing by

we learn to live with ourselves

VIII. PRINCIPLES

on occasion
we must be nothing
and take time to breathe
before diving back

We do not need affirmation and become immune to false judgment when we understand and become harmonious within our self.

When life knocks the stuffing out of you like a plush toy, remember your shape is still there. All it takes is some new stuffing and sewing.

not all rocks

are meant to be

cast into walls

we may have weaknesses

but they will only be cured

by seeing and using our strengths

Find out and be circumspect.

we are filaments

in an incandescent universe

VIII. PRINCIPLES

come to your senses
imagine those missing
and feel the universe

Youth has imprudent aspects but also carries an innocent conscience against perversions of age. Mutual learning and respect are necessary.

"Be who you are" may be falsely interpreted as advising complacency. To realize opportunities for improvement, we must question ourselves and everything else.

we need only what we need
too much can be as vile
as too little

hooks in our life
we won't excise
pull tighter and keep us in check

different traits and talents
provide interest and balance

In stillness we meet our self.

humans
longing
not built
to just be

Sudden improvements in the human condition could be achieved if more people decided to be careful with the hearts of others - and their own.

"You can do anything if you put your mind to it" is obvious nonsense. But you won't know what you can attain unless you put your mind to it.

The strength of a man includes self-restraint and knowing when to let go.

i will respect
i will not permit denial of respect
social ground rules

All we wish to receive from others we must be willing to give.

Negative attitude inescapably foreshadows negative results.

VIII. PRINCIPLES

works in progress

don't want to be finished

only assured we are on the right path

The world is a filled waiting room not expecting us.

The point of activities is to a point engaging in them.

Forgiving people what they think, feel, or do better include the future.

instead of saying
what i would not give
give and see what happens

Hunger for life cannot be stilled by possessions. Experiences and advancements of ulterior purposes are necessary. But why would we want to be satisfied in any event?

Enough babble of only the present counting. The past has brought us and our setting to where we are. By ignoring it, we fail shaping the future.

VIII. PRINCIPLES

consider that all passes
let it come and go
toward a better future

Admonitions to smile may sound naive, but positive body language opens doors for rational and emotional communication and consideration in us and others.

Expressing what we want by exclusion is exceedingly more cumbersome and less motivating than stating it positively.

"Perception is reality" is the epitome of cynicism and absurdity. It is like saying "the truth is whatever someone deems it to be." This would mean no one could be mistaken.

life is not fair
but isn't humanity about
making it fairer

People who claim they would change nothing if they could relive their life lie or suffer a total absence of critical thinking and imagination.

VIII. PRINCIPLES

Be like a tree on the coast. Grow with the wind, and you will persist. Unless the wind changes. Then your best hope is reincarnation.

Be like water in a stream. There, one cannot tell whether it flushes or is flushed. Humanity moves like that. Thus, no extra effort is required.

Be like a lotus. Tethered, to your neck in stale water, unseen creatures brushing up, you feeding on their muck. But at least you look great.

When we blame circumstances and others for holding us back, we may use them as scapegoats for our lack of courage to actualize our aspirations.

Positive attitude is a motivating and possibly necessary bias. But how can we attain or retain happiness without analyzing what is or could go wrong?

fearless but humble
ambitious but loving
realistic but hopeful
engaged but calm

VIII. PRINCIPLES

"Live every day as if it were your last" is idiotic advice. Individuals and societies would utterly fall apart if they heeded it. Instead, we should see each day as an opportunity for constructive progress and, if necessary, new beginnings.

empty everything
sort consider arrange
keep only what you need

Sometimes we have to go out of our way to find it.

to understand things
we must become them
the same applies to us

Seven billion have enough power to
help one another everywhere.

There is ample employment in
improving our world.

Destruction is a reaction to
frustration from lack of movement.

VIII. PRINCIPLES

"Never give up" is a foolish suggestion. We must constantly reevaluate the effectiveness and efficiencies of our courses of action as well as the proprieties of objectives.

everything we try to prove
we must try to disprove as well

Views regarding principles of human conduct change with perceptions of their utility. As a consequence, no rule may be respected forever unless its acceptance can be firmly settled.

one cannot live dreams

without truth setting in

the honesty of practice

forced results

rarely last

and threaten to cost

more than is gained

Human pursuits could dramatically benefit from focusing reactions to frustrations on their causes and by a strict dedication to resolving them most effectively and efficiently.

IX. LIFE AND DEATH

IX. LIFE AND DEATH

There was and will be a very long time without your existence. Make this precious interval of being fully count by living a happy life.

we once were not
and soon
will not be again
we better be happy then

Multiply the years you have reasonably left by 12 months. This gives you a better idea of how little time there is to make the best of life.

forgive forget forge ahead

don't die for a lifetime

break all decency of mourning

far away

from what we wanted

until death

our life will be haunted

by all factors that brought us here

as much as we try

to elude and fight death

its shadow follows us

until we merge into it

IX. LIFE AND DEATH

the ill orange tree
grew blossoms
out of season
as a last act of beauty
in the throws of
its fight for life

To weather life's storms and make
sense of it, we must first understand
and become centered in ourselves.

a well-lived life is
about not taking
anybody's word for it

some of us refuse

starting something new

even if it seems appealing

as if they would get

that chance in another life

there are days . . .

stop right there

and be glad about that

freezing time

is like holding your breath

you can't do it for long

without dying

IX. LIFE AND DEATH

a ladder
with rungs missing
and questions where it leads

life is sho –

some leave
never having been there

having checked all systems
still falling from the sky
pilot says calmly goodbye

that all times will end
source of hope
and pain

most tired of living
before they die
regrets still burn deeply
when it is time

So what if you're damaged. We all
are, and our impairments die with us.
But we are still here, holding the
most precious gift in our hands. Any
damage cannot much affect its luster.

IX. LIFE AND DEATH

Identifying worthy pursuits gains a necessary dimension of support from learning about detrimental pursuits. Their distinctions define one another.

If we cannot live on in our awareness, we wish to live on in other persons' minds. But what are we doing to deserve such an important status?

After we are gone, someone may experience something of us and wonder about its context and who we were. Our dearest wish is to tell them.

We may not be able to grasp life while being immersed in it. Clarity may only set in as it draws to its end.

We fear death if we imagine an afterlife aware without a body, in a decaying body, or subject to other limits on happiness. To curb such horrors, we create fantasies of moving on to another life with similar or superior opportunities for happiness.

Until death, we may not deem our existence a matter of life and death.

IX. LIFE AND DEATH

most people defer

deeper considerations

until death impends

as if preparing for a test

on a subject they hate

but tragically it is then too late

they lived and died

nobody bothered

neither had they

what if this is about

the waiting hall

not the boarding of a train

my sadness about dying
mellowed by assurances
nature is only sleeping

Our lives are plagued by our inability to change the past and by death. How can we make the best of this?

The average human lifetime is just long enough to fully experience the contest and ultimately resounding and permanent crushing of a child's sunny disposition and high hopes. Our assignment is to change that.

IX. LIFE AND DEATH

how to live

to not be sorry

and not to worry

we naturally imagine

life like a day

born to fresh dawn

tiring at dusk

waking again

after a night's rest

childishly seeking confirmation

life is a teacher

insisting all lessons be paid

ultimately we cannot
think feel believe talk or act
our way out of this life or its end

We cannot imagine not being.

all that is gained
all that is paid or lost
is life a zero sum game or worse

moving forward without completion
is in the nature of being alive

IX. LIFE AND DEATH

back when i was
i was unaware
had better things to do
now that i'm not
if i could feel
i'd feel an endless rue

we all are time races in the end
ash sludge bleached bones
then environment

who or what causes you
to dissipate your life
inquire and cancel your permission

am i whole

what am i missing

we must answer unpleasant questions

wake up

days are not waiting

embrace each one lovingly

reminders spurned

by the aloof

ravenous people

like paging ahead

forgetting

turned leaves will be gone

X.
FREEDOM

X. FREEDOM

When you lose everything but yourself you are truly free. Unless you need anything beyond yourself.

Everything we have possesses us in turn. Therefore, losing or giving away what we have may not be all bad. It liberates us to make a new beginning.

Individual freedom to do as one pleases has developed a bad reputation from its irresponsible exercise and from forceful struggles involving its suppression.

she acts out
all her ages

After exposure to external and
internal directives, suggestions, and
doubts, what is left of us? Can we
define ourselves, or are we defined?

leaders are dealers
in fear and attraction
you will be tethered
to their plan of action
unless you stay free
to reject or agree

X. FREEDOM

Instead of hierarchies based on power differentials, human development requires functional organization reflecting ongoing consensual entrustment according to capabilities.

Leadership implies submission. Can we mature and replace this archaic concept with shared vision to which participants deliberately contribute?

the wind believes
in the loyalty
of weather vanes

Neither be a leader nor a follower.
Both are demeaning. We all look for
paths to happiness. Let us learn,
work, and share with one another.

Praisers of leadership demonstrate
confusion about the direction of
human evolution and failure to learn
from hierarchy's disastrous past or
inferior effectiveness and efficiency.

not holding what
does not want to be held
or better is left unkept

X. FREEDOM

brutalizers claim
the right of the stronger
as ordering principle
most others agree
and learn their language

the dancer left the music box
tired of spinning in place
to the same tune
bolted to the ground
for the amusement
of anyone winding her up

instinct hard to overcome by learning

We must decide how much we wish to find who we are, remain true to the state we find, or reconcile it more.

The world is still a welcoming place for people who like to tell others what to do and those who take orders. This hierarchic tradition refutes human dignity expressed in harmonic needs. Peace cannot endure until it ends.

If nobody had power over anybody, everybody would be free, requiring responsible exercise or restriction.

X. FREEDOM

As long as we seek or accept power over others, or grant or concede such power to others, we and humanity will remain stuck in primitivity.

Democracy is an imperfect form of social organization because it legalizes the replacement of harmonization with the dictates of majorities over those losing a vote.

The idea of a fair society is agreement on its affairs as well as awareness and upholding of fundamental rights.

Being governed by 1%, 51%, or any other fraction may differ little for those overpowered. Harmonization is the only remedy for despotism.

Humanity will not heal as long as we define success as superiority over others. Societies engendering winners and losers continue to be endlessly plagued by contempt and anguish.

if all suffering injustice
would act up
it could not exist

X. FREEDOM

looking back
our years are like days
and still we are patiently
walking the maze
instead of cutting through

you are only free
if you can pack up and leave
choose commitments wisely

we find our self
back
somewhere
before compliance training

Cooperation encourages the best in us, competition the worst.

Competition cannot match the effectiveness, efficiency, and humaneness of cooperation.

we want to run away
but do not have a way
or other part to play
so we stay
incarcerating feelings
rearranging dealings
to fight another day

X. FREEDOM

i could not tame her
nor would i try
to blame or shame her
she'd never comply
i want her free
to run with me

Attempts to stop movement around us may vary in their success, but they inevitably restrict our own mobility.

raptured frustration
a long-time gestation
of who we are in extremes

Mistreating people for disagreeing
will not convince them we are right.

running wild
in forlorn gardens
lairs of branches
paths in tall grass
children play
until fantasy hardens
will they recall
how precious it was

The most insidious form of free
speech suppression is self-censorship.

X. FREEDOM

layers of mantles
chains of locks
still her spirit
roamed free

Freedom is justified by allowing us to arrange our life for best happiness. Its limit is the requirement of internal and external harmonization, a crucial ingredient of our happiness.

Our and other persons' freedom must be restricted to achieve optimized harmony among fundamental rights.

we separate from nature

wishing to be united

distance from childhood

to recapture its wonder

sacrifice our hearts

bemoaning incompleteness

We invest enormous efforts building security in patterns only to feel caught in their mesh.

Most human settings require and accommodate dullness, torturing the aware. Development may change this.

X. FREEDOM

was self-awareness

introspection by her body

or looking out of

a living shell

was she a high expression of nature

or a spirit to briefly dwell

driven people

passengers

of their obsessions

crushed fill on the road

for the heinous

unless we assert ourselves

when too much

wants a piece of us

or tries to become a piece

we must defend

our entirety's peace

what happened to us

easier to admit than

what we let happen to us

People are increasingly in the
enviable position of being able to do
what they want - if they only wanted
to find out and do what they want.

X. FREEDOM

We cannot take possession of our existence until we sense, think, and feel it through. Anything short of this exposes us to being lost or possessed.

she was determined
to stop wasting time
explore life from then on
free of assumptions

The secret of securing privilege is to render subjects concerned about losing their possessions and make the privileged appear to be guarantors.

We will never be entirely free because the satisfaction of our needs requires engagements. The most we should expect is being able to select and deselect attachments we desire.

Those wishing to restrict conduct not unduly impacting fundamental rights are trying to share the pain of their own restrictions or to take advantage.

we will never be free
until we release
what we do not dare to express

www.ingramcontent.com/pod-product-compliance
Lightning Source LLC
Chambersburg PA
CBHW032109090426
42743CB00007B/290